HAL•LEONARD GUITAR PLAY-ALONG

POP/ROCK

CONTENTS

Tracking, mixing, and mastering by Jake Johnson
All guitars by Doug Boduch
Bass by Tom McGirr
Keyboards by Warren Wiegratz
Drums by Scott Schroedl

ISBN 0-634-05622-0

Visit Hal Leonard Online at www.halleonard.com

This book not for sale in the E.U.

HAL•LEONARD®
CORPORATION
7777 W. BLUEMOUND RD. P.O. BOX 13819
MILWAUKEE, WISCONSIN 53213

Breakdown

Words and Music by Tom Petty

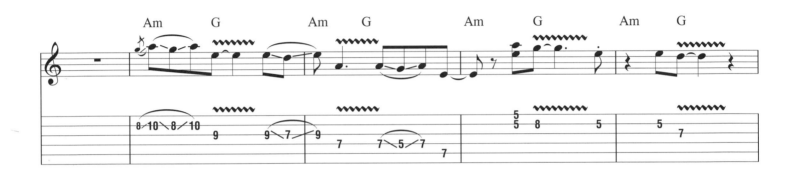

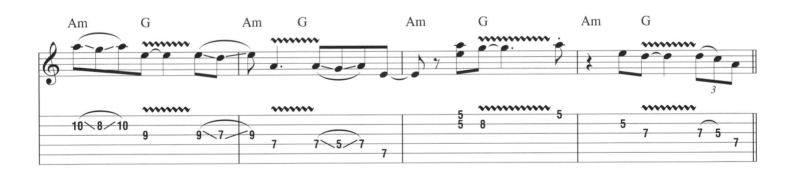

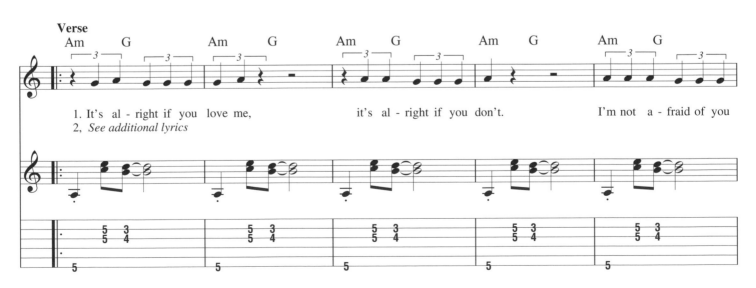

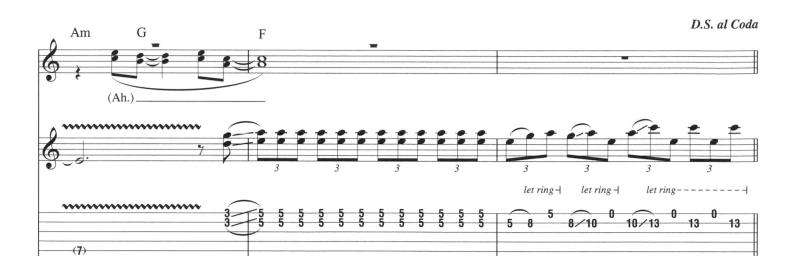

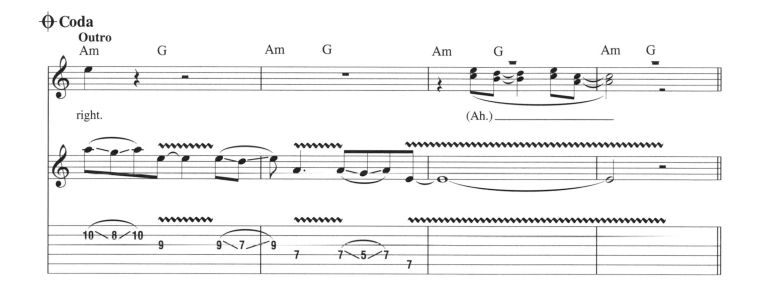

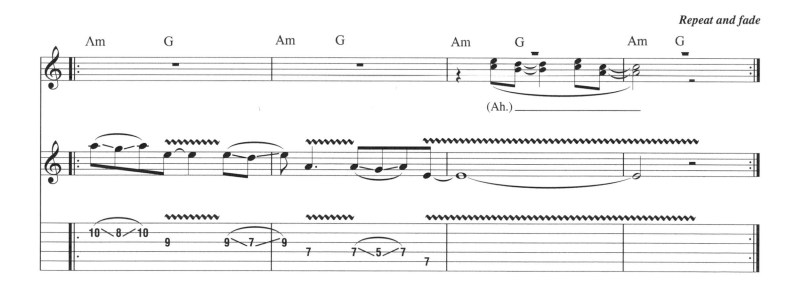

Additional Lyrics

2. There is no sense in pretending;
   Your eyes give you away.
   Somethin' inside you is feelin' like I do.
   We've said all there is to say.

Crazy Little Thing Called Love

Words and Music by Freddie Mercury

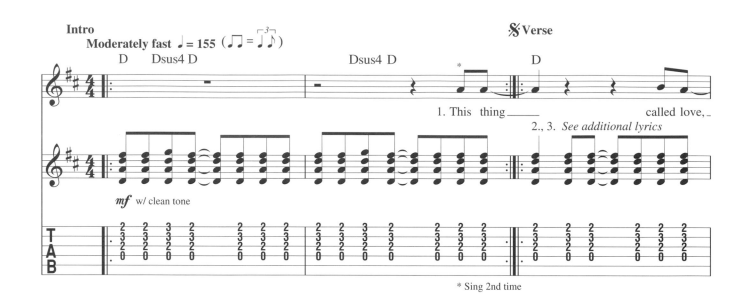

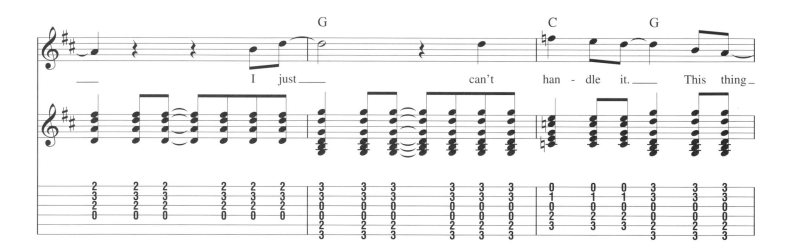

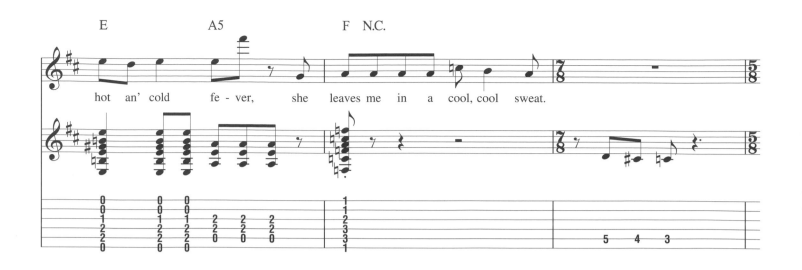

hot an' cold fe - ver, she leaves me in a cool, cool sweat.

D.S. al Coda 1

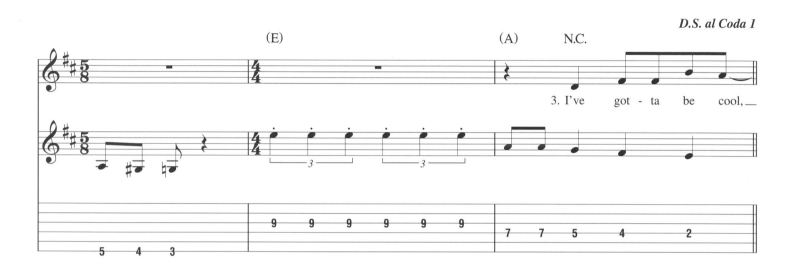

3. I've got - ta be cool, ___

⊕ Coda 1

Guitar Solo

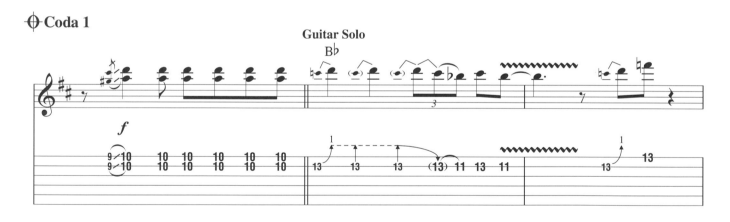

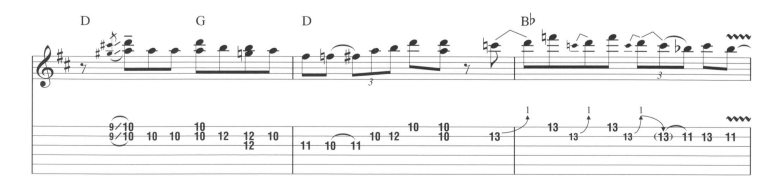

Additional Lyrics

2. A this thing called love
   It cries in a cradle all night.
   It swings, it jives,
   Shakes all over like a jellyfish.
   I kinda like it.
   Crazy little thing called love.

3. I've gotta be cool, relax,
   Get hip, get on my tracks.
   Take a back seat, hitchhike,
   Take a long ride on my motorbike
   Until I'm ready.
   Crazy little thing called love.

Hit Me With Your Best Shot

Words and Music by Eddie Schwartz

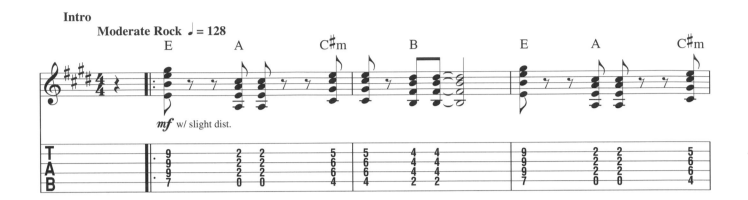

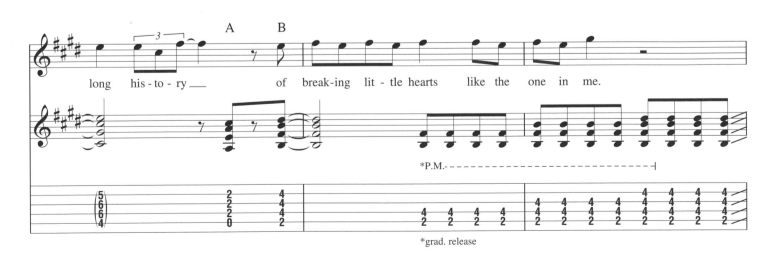

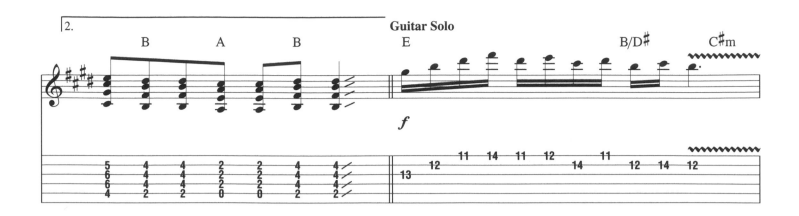

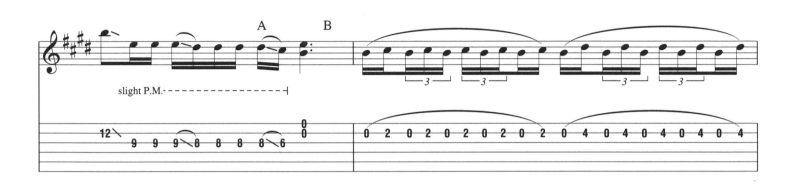

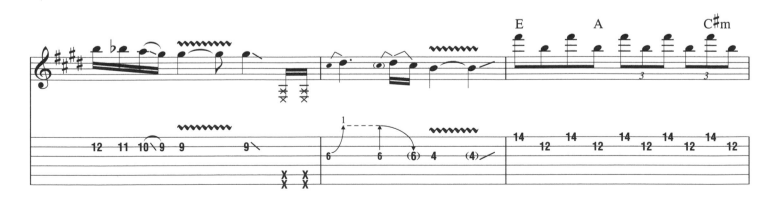

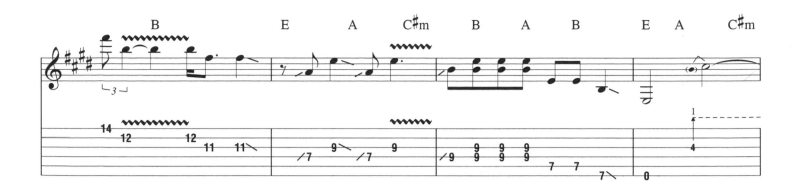

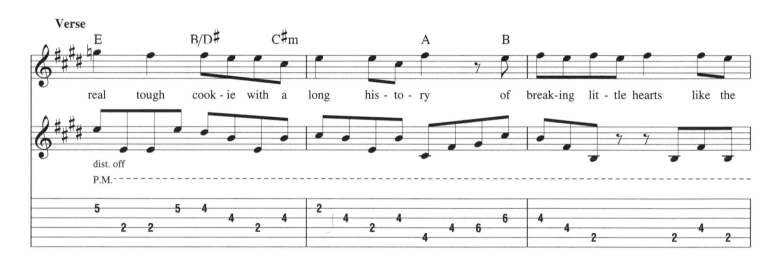

3. Well, you're a

Verse

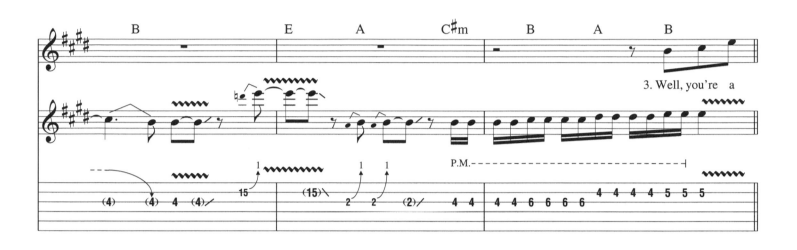

real tough cook - ie with a   long   his - to - ry   of   break - ing   lit - tle hearts   like the

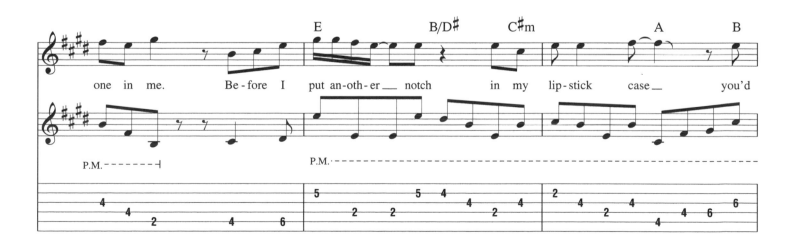

one in me.   Be - fore I   put an - oth - er __ notch   in my   lip - stick   case __   you'd

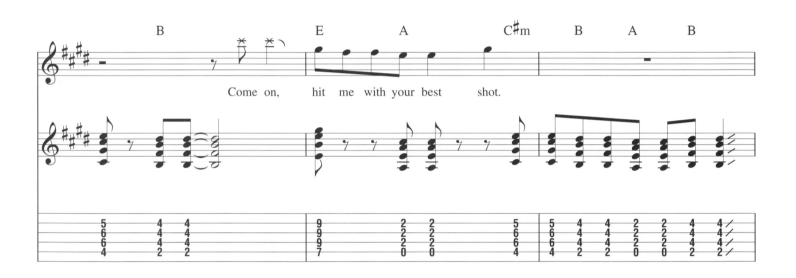

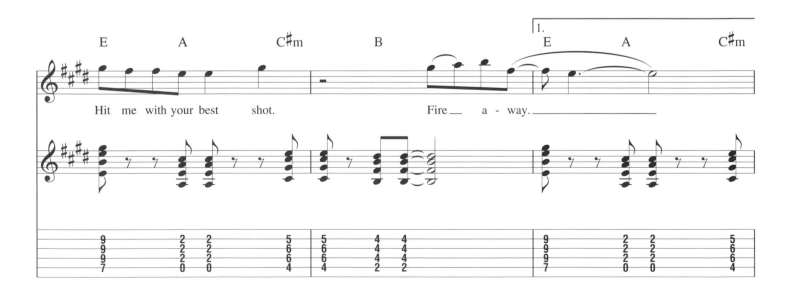

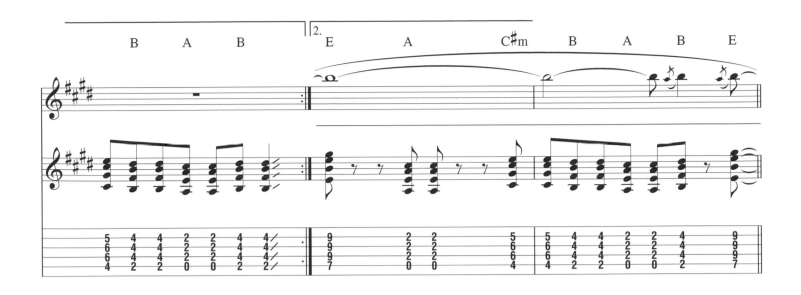

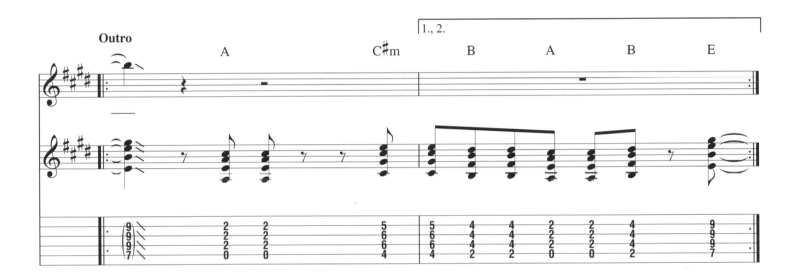

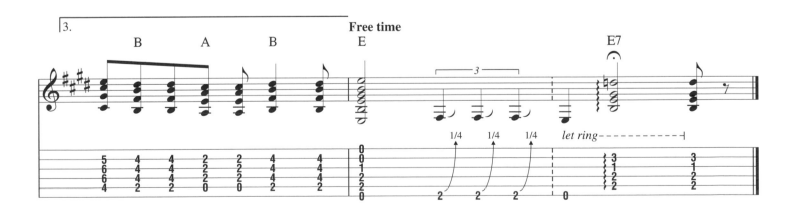

Additional Lyrics

2. You come on with a come on, you don't fight fair.
   But that's O.K., see if I care.
   Knock me down, it's all in vain.
   I'll get right back on my feet again.

I Want You to Want Me

Words and Music by Rick Nielsen

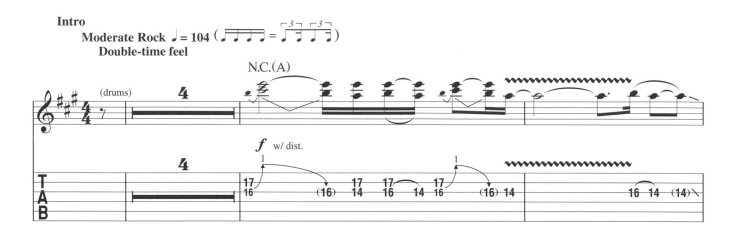

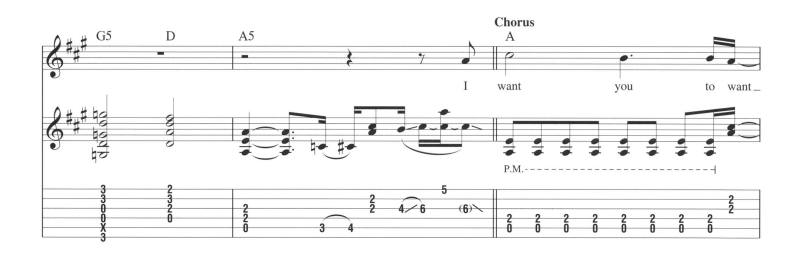

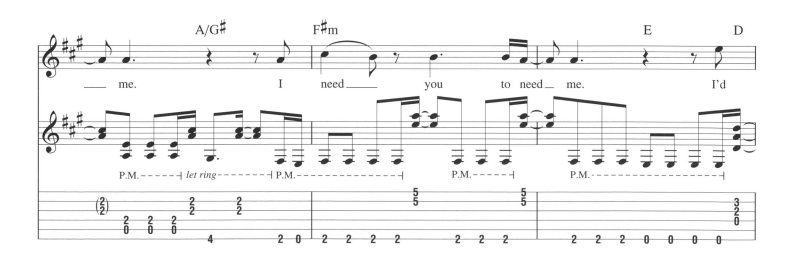

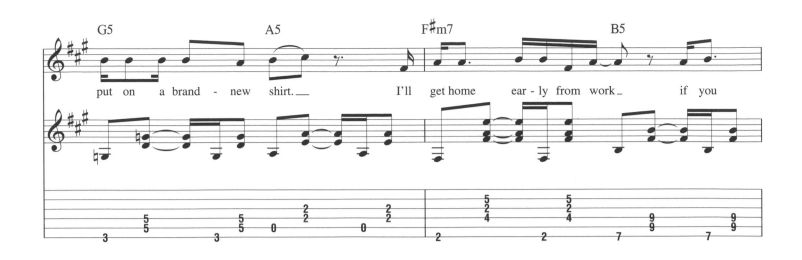

put on a brand - new shirt. ___ I'll get home ear - ly from work ___ if you

D.S. al Coda

say that you love ___ me.

Coda

Guitar Solo

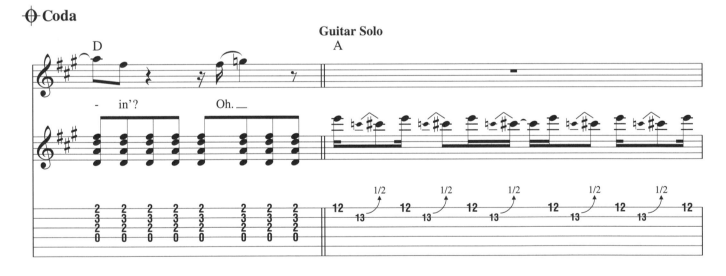

- in'? Oh. ___

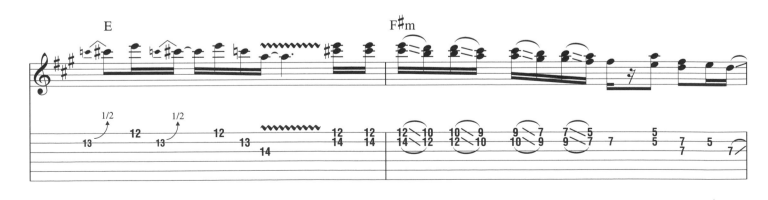

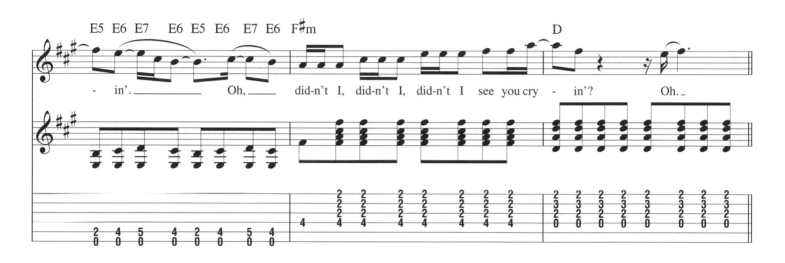

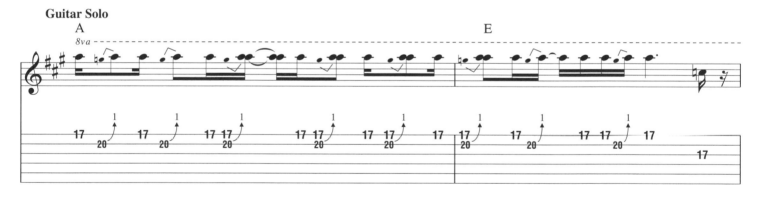

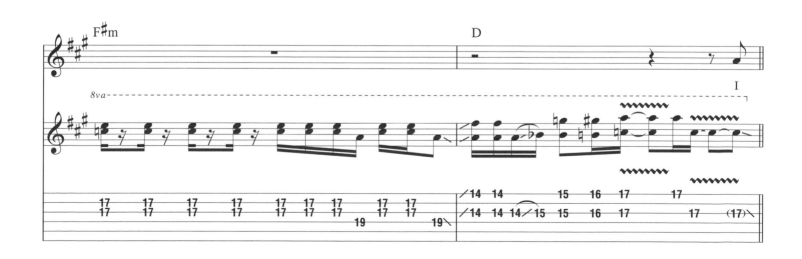

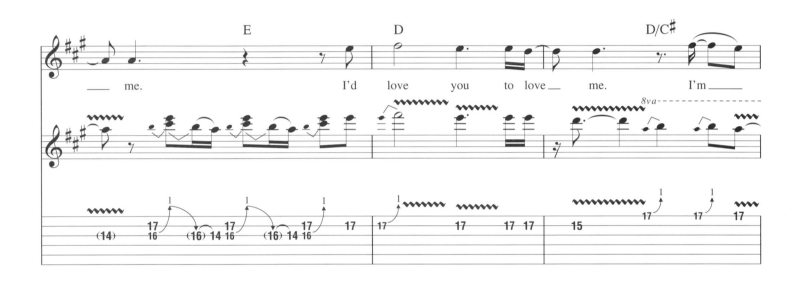

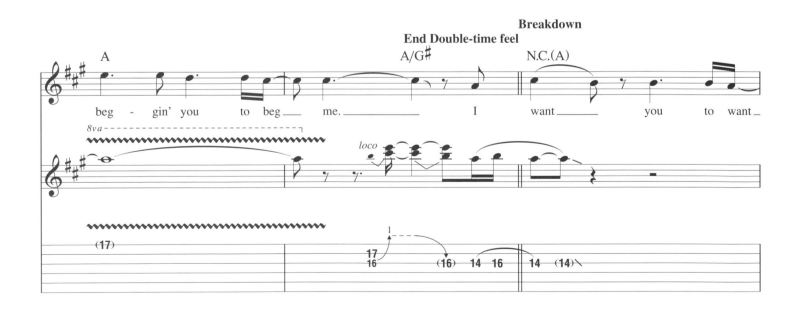

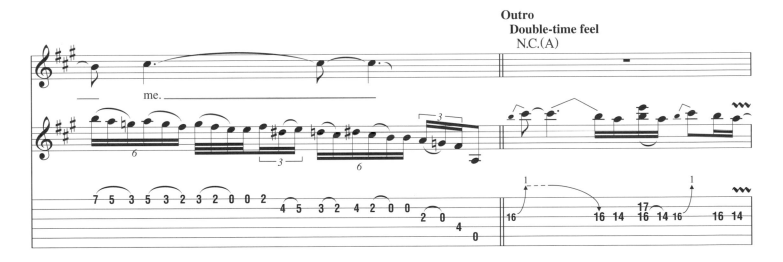

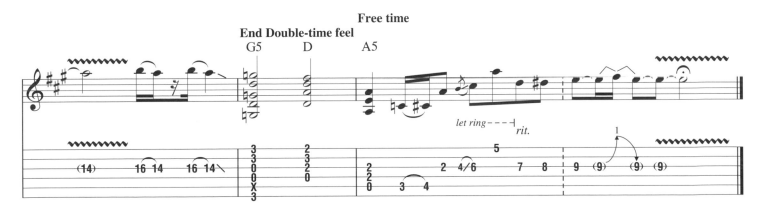

Lights

Words and Music by Steve Perry and Neal Schon

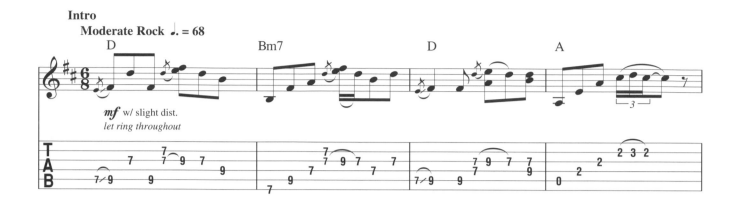

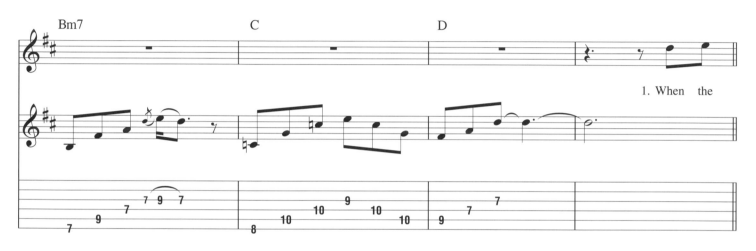

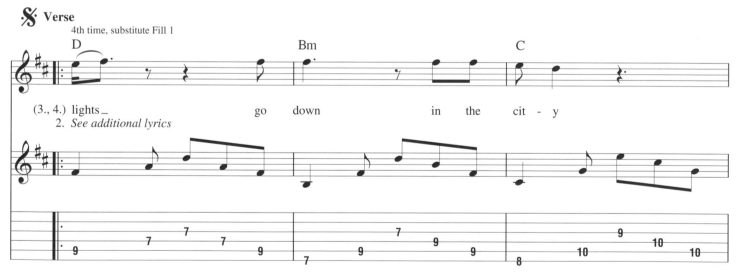

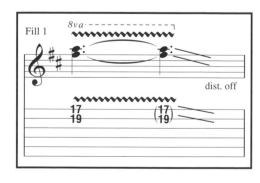

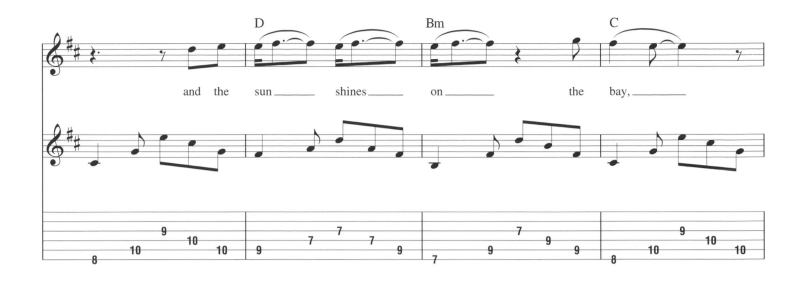

and the sun____ shines____ on____ the bay,____

oo, I wan - na be there_____ in my____ cit - y.

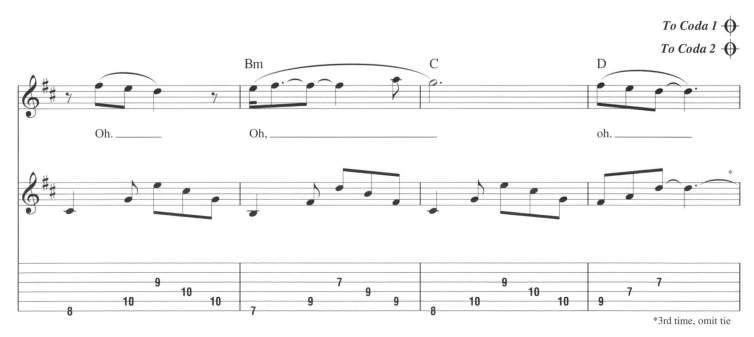

To Coda 1 ⊕
To Coda 2 ⊕

Oh._____ Oh,____ oh._____

*3rd time, omit tie

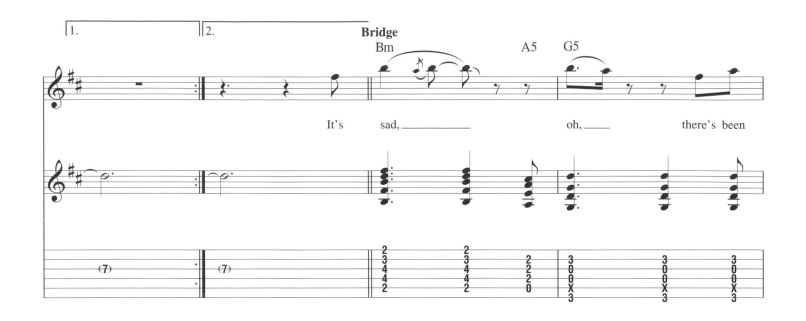

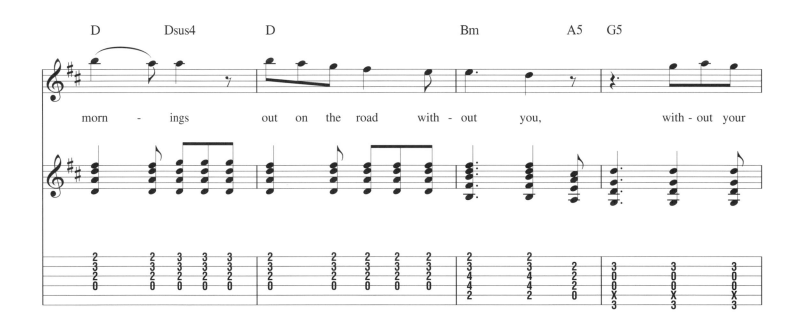

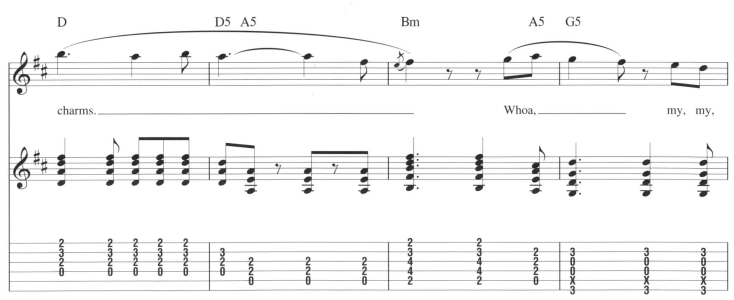

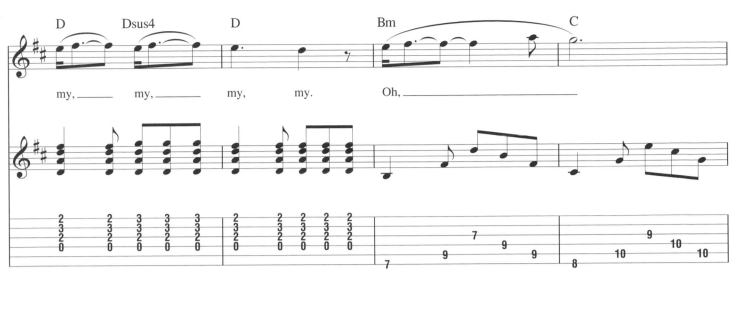

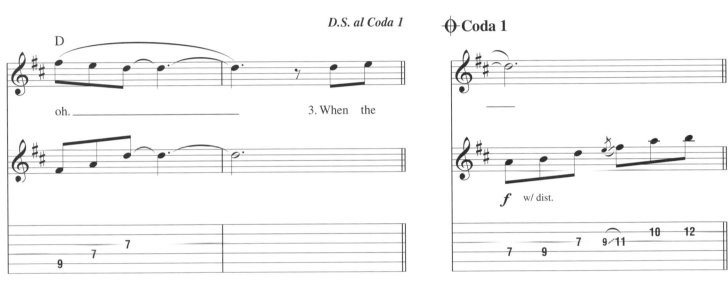

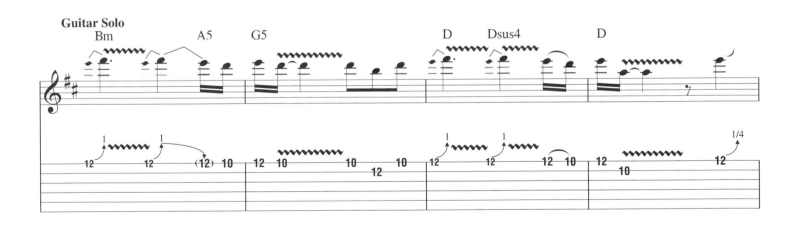

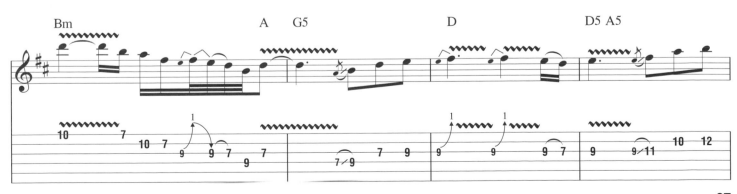

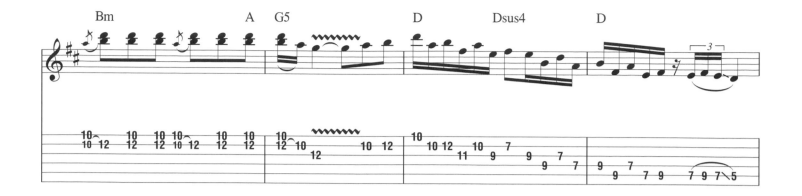

D.S. al Coda 2

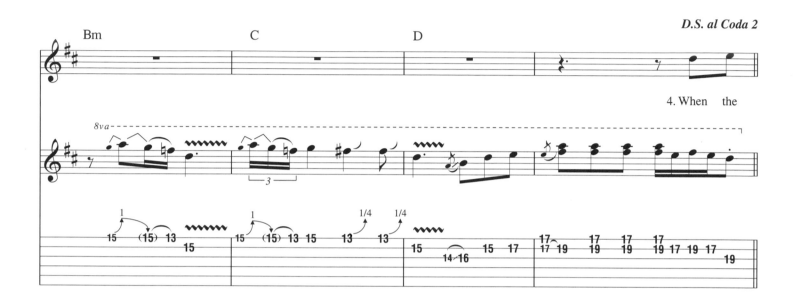

4. When the

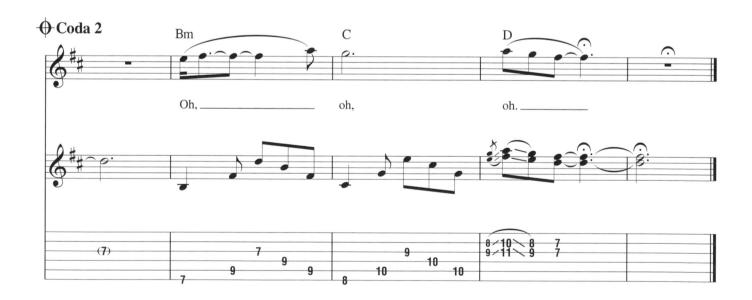

Oh, _____ oh, _____ oh. _____

Additional Lyrics

2. So you think you're lonely.
   Well, my friend, I'm lonely too.
   I want to get back to my city by the bay.
   Whoa, oh, oh.

R.O.C.K. in the U.S.A.
(A Salute to 60's Rock)

Words and Music by John Mellencamp

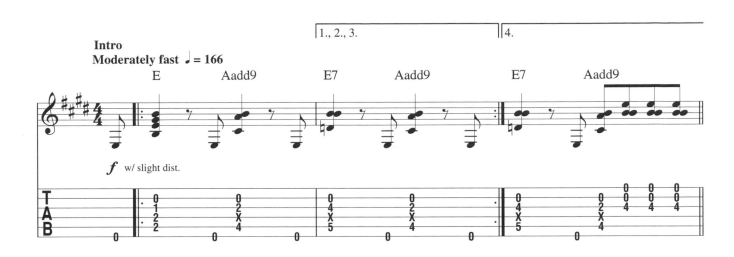

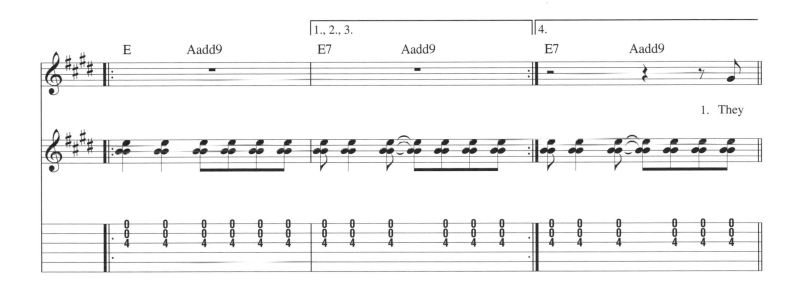

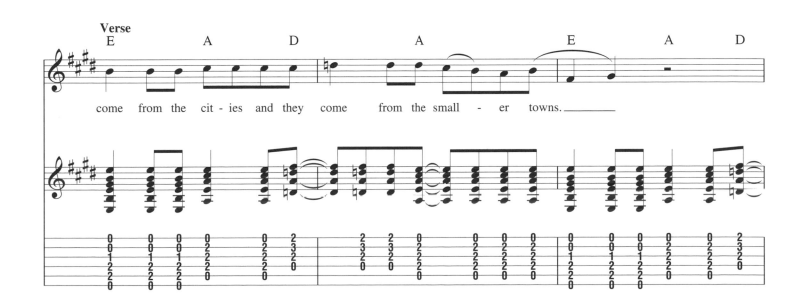

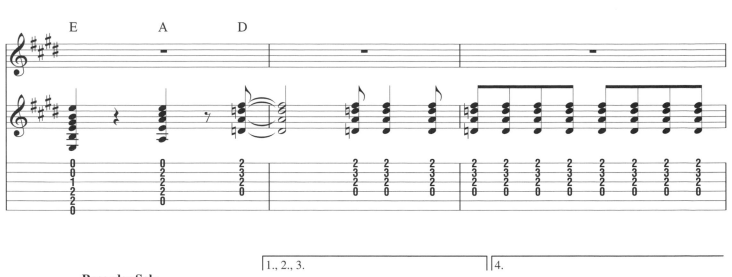

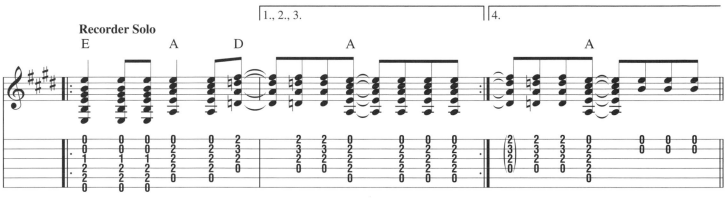

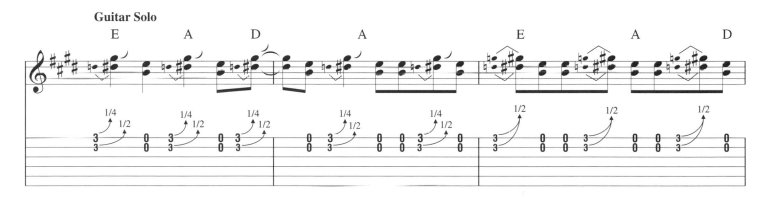

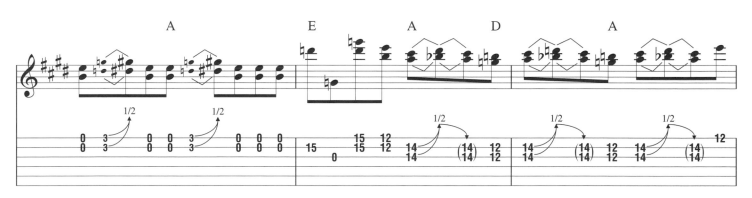

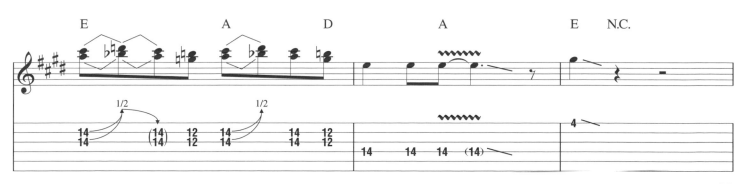

Summer of '69

Words and Music by Bryan Adams and Jim Vallance

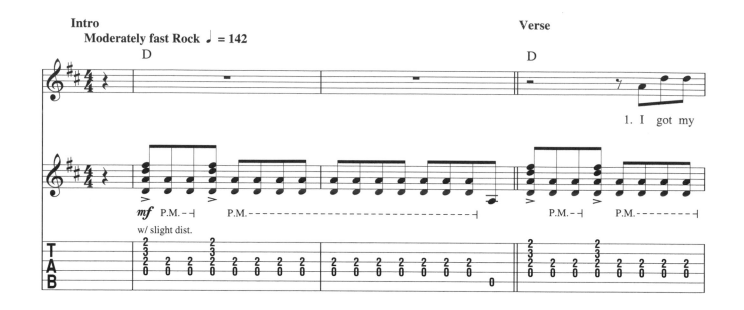

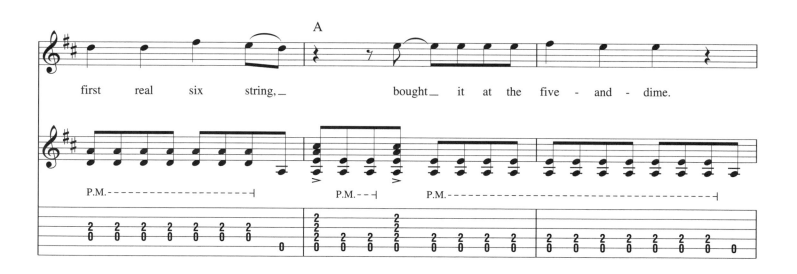

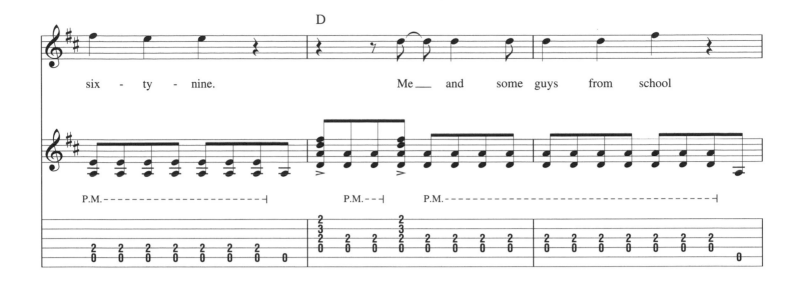

six - ty - nine. Me__ and some guys from school

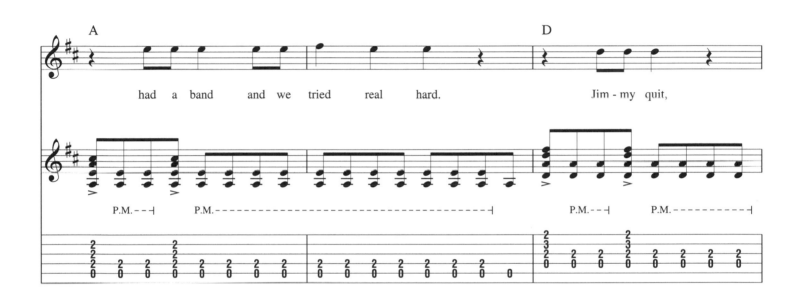

had a band and we tried real hard. Jim - my quit,

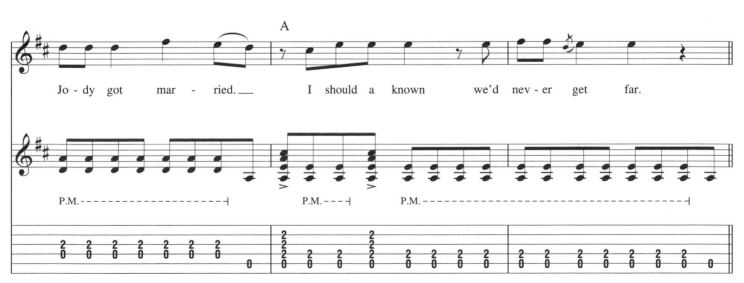

Jo - dy got mar - ried.__ I should a known we'd nev - er get far.

Pre-Chorus

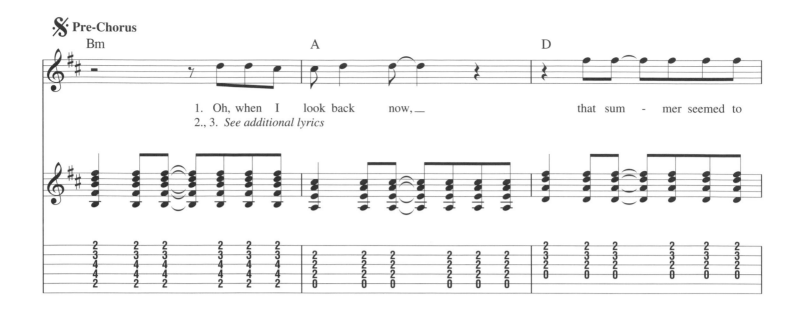

1. Oh, when I look back now,— that sum - mer seemed to
2., 3. *See additional lyrics*

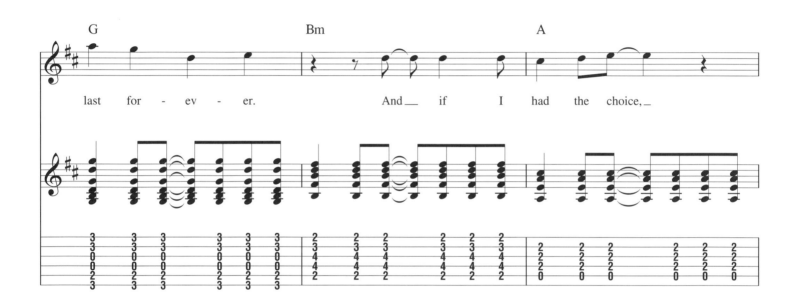

last for - ev - er. And — if I had the choice,—

yeah,— I'd al - ways wan - na be there. Those — were the

38

To Coda 1

To Coda 2

Interlude

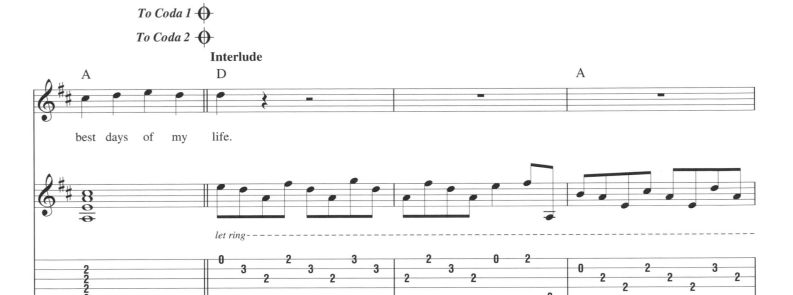

best days of my life.

let ring

Verse

Yeah.

2. Ain't no use ___ in com-plain - in' ___

let ring   P.M.   P.M.

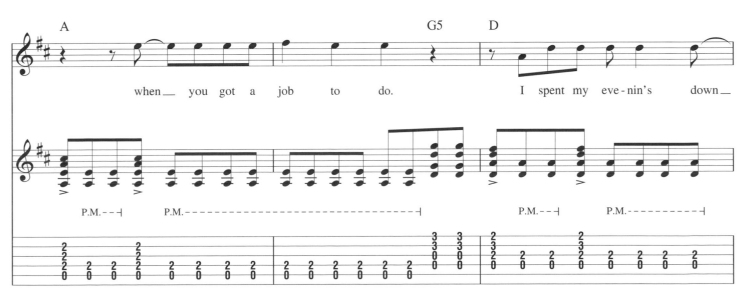

when ___ you got a job to do.   I spent my eve-nin's down ___

P.M.   P.M.   P.M.   P.M.

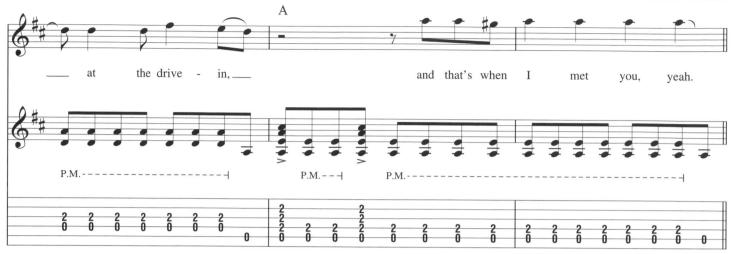

at the drive - in, ___ and that's when I met you, yeah.

Coda 1

Chorus

life. Oh, ___ yeah. ___

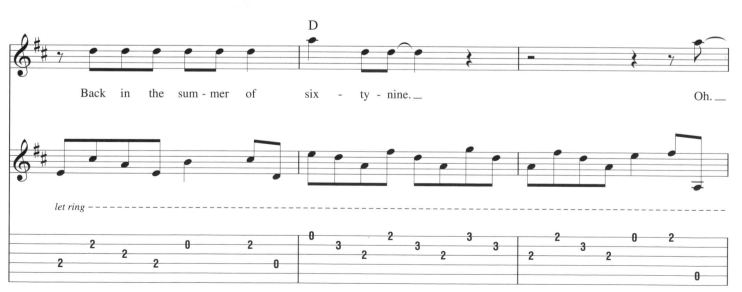

Back in the sum - mer of six - ty - nine. ___ Oh. ___

Verse

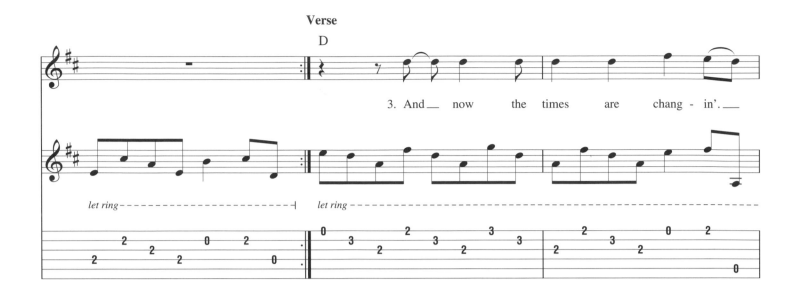

3. And__ now the times are chang-in'.__

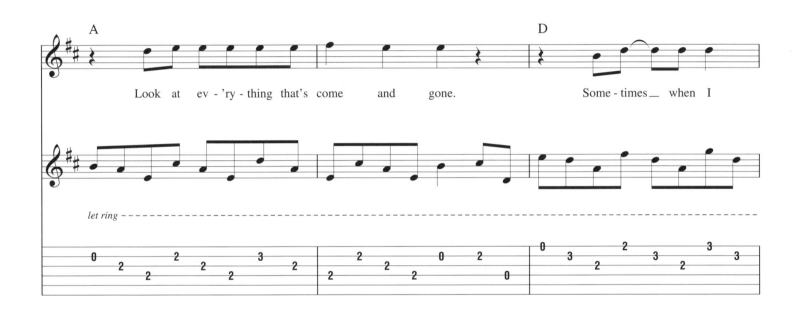

Look at ev-'ry-thing that's come and gone. Some-times__ when I

D.S. al Coda 2

play that old six-string,__ think a-bout ya, won-der what went wrong.

⊕ Coda 2

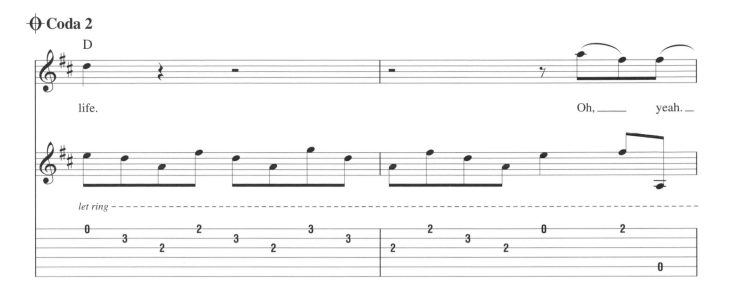

life.   Oh, _____ yeah. _____

Outro

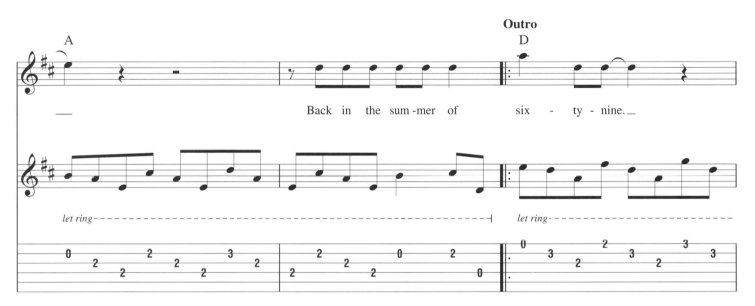

___   Back in the sum-mer of   six - ty - nine. _____

Repeat and fade

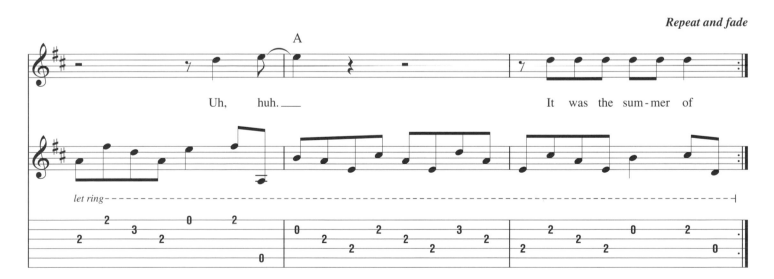

Uh,   huh. _____   It was the sum-mer of

Additional Lyrics

Pre-Chorus 2., 3. Standin' on your mama's porch

You told me that { you'd wait / it'd last } forever.

Oh, and when you held my hand,
I knew that it was now or never.
Those were the best days of my life.

What I Like About You

Words and Music by Michael Skill, Wally Palamarchuk and James Marinos

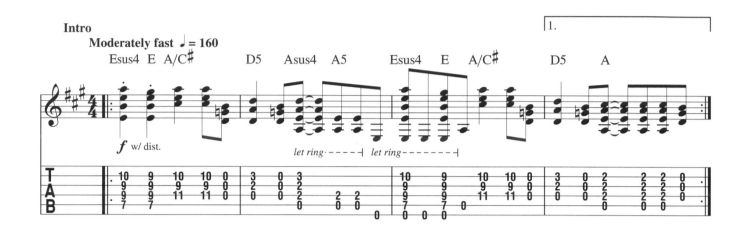

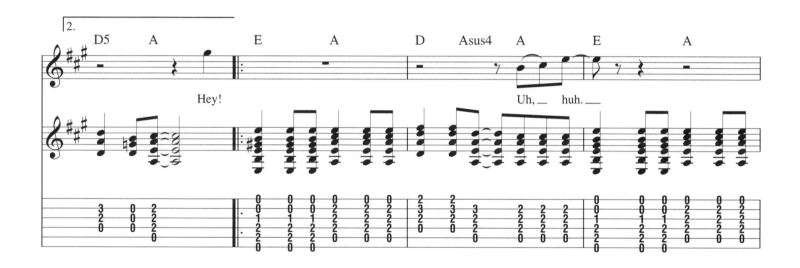

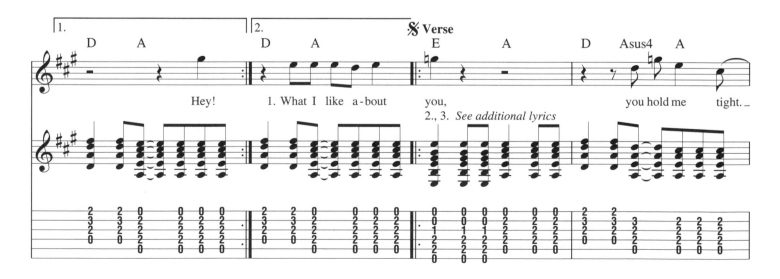

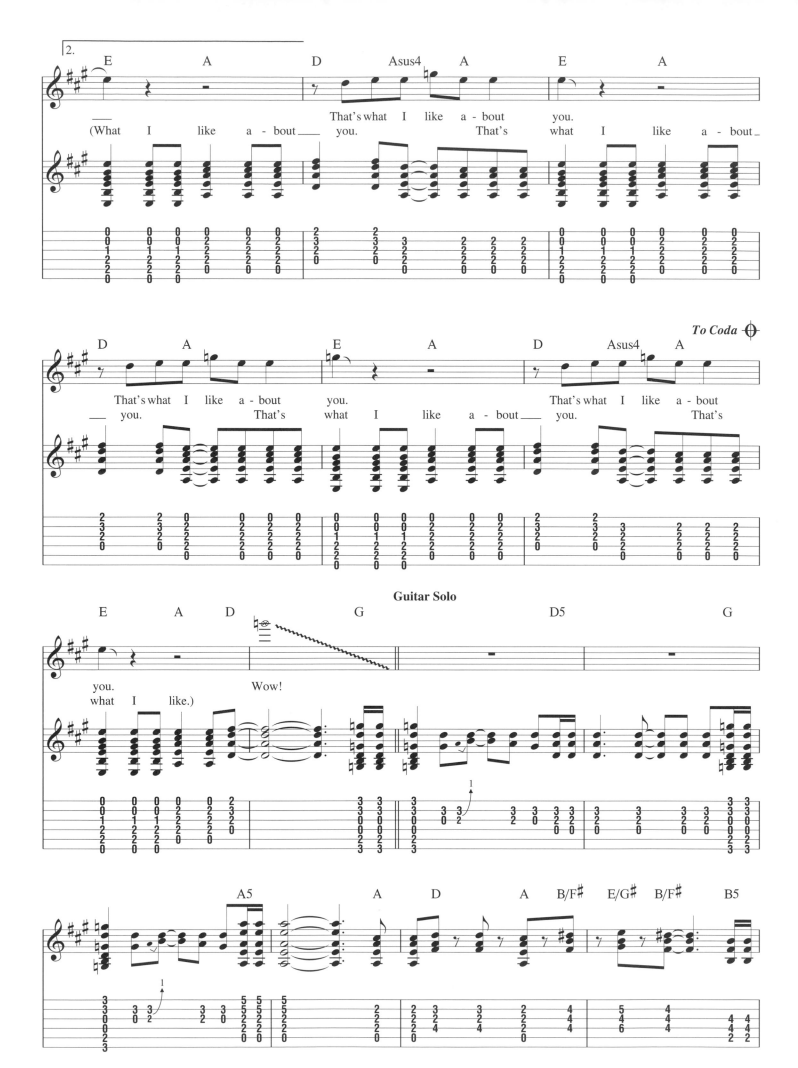

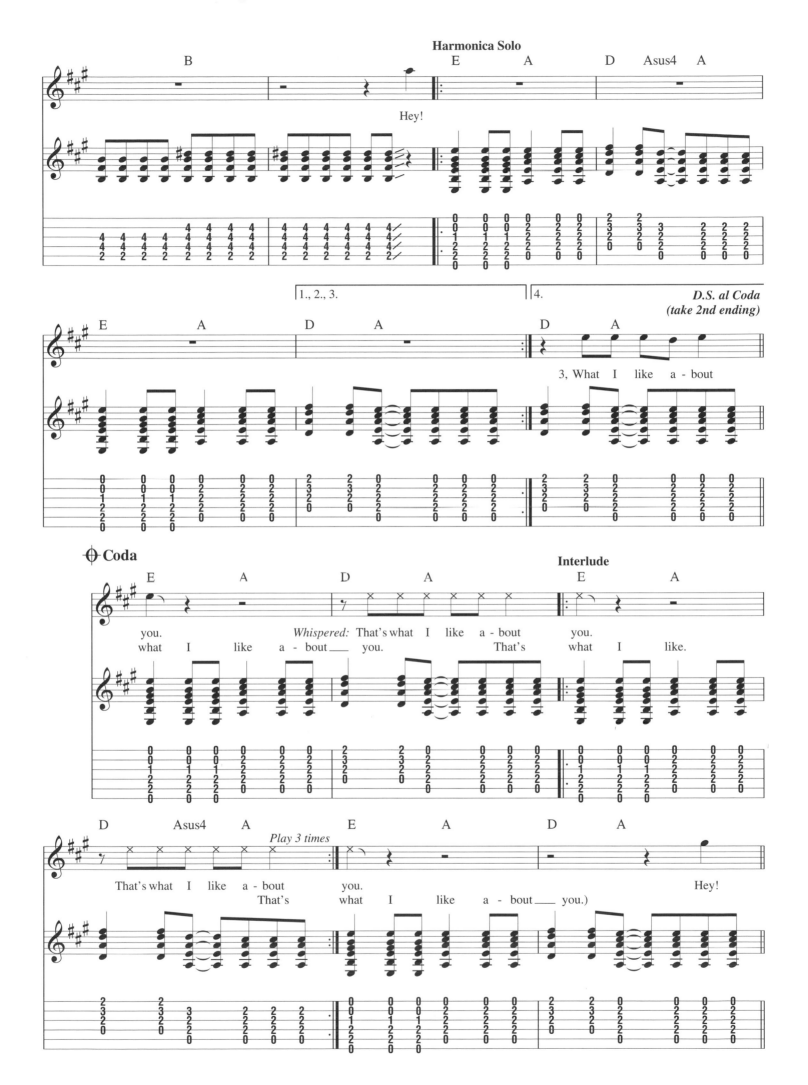

Outro

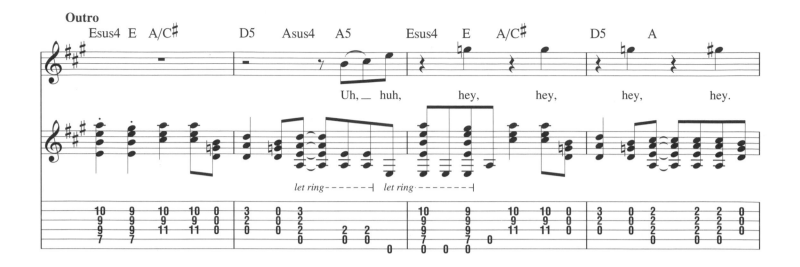

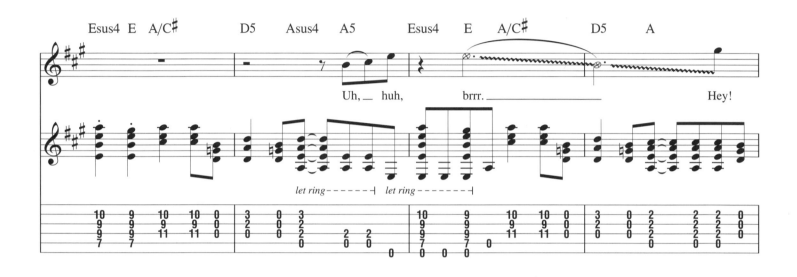

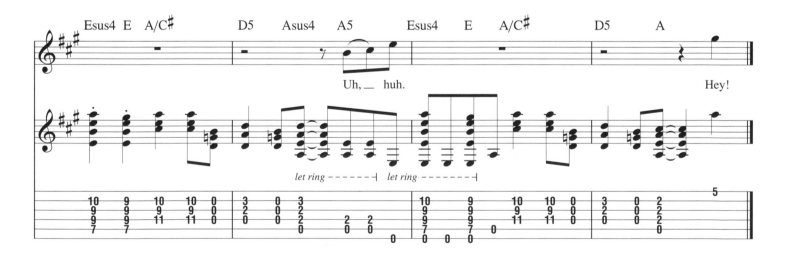

Additional Lyrics

2. What I like about you,
   You really know how to dance.
   When you go uptown jump around,
   Think about true romance. Yeah.

3. What I like about you,
   You keep me warm at night.
   Never wanna let you go,
   Know you make me feel alright. Yeah.